JAMES MARTIN

LIVING FOSSILS

ANIMALS THAT HAVE WITHSTOOD THE TEST OF TIME

ILLUSTRATED WITH PHOTOGRAPHS · PAINTINGS BY JANET HAMLIN

CROWN PUBLISHERS, INC., NEW YORK

For Mickie and Willy — J.M.

Text copyright © 1997 by James Martin
Illustrations copyright © 1997 by Janet Hamlin

Photographic acknowledgments:
Thomas C. Boyden: 11 *top*
Nigel Catlin/Holt Studios International: 43, 46
Bruce Davidson/Animals Animals: 33
Douglas Faulkner: 17
Delores R. Fernandes & Michael L. Peck: 31 *center right*, 37
H. Fricke: 22, 26
James Martin: 1, 4, 10, 18, 27, 30, 31 *top,*
32, 36, 38, 39, 44, 45 *top & center,* 47
Joe McDonald: 12, 13
John L. Pontier/Animals Animals: 45 *bottom*
J. Schauer/Fricke: 23
Donald Specker/Animals Animals: 11 *bottom*

Published by Crown Publishers, Inc., a Random House company, 201 East 50th Street,
New York, New York 10022

CROWN is a trademark of Crown Publishers, Inc.

Printed in Hong Kong
http://www.randomhouse.com/

Library of Congress Cataloging-in-Publication Data
Martin, James, 1950–
Living fossils / by James Martin.
p.   cm.
Includes index.
1. Living fossils—Juvenile literature. [1. Living fossils.] I. Title.
QL85.5.M37   1997   591—dc20   94-7926

ISBN 0-517-59866-3 (trade)
ISBN 0-517-59867-1 (lib. bdg.)

10 9 8 7 6 5 4 3 2 1

First Edition

The Earth's Geological History

Each of the seven living fossils
described in this book is shown below
in the time period when its ancestors
first lived. The letters "mya" stand for
millions of years ago.

page 10   page 14   page 40

CAMBRIAN	ORDOVICIAN	SILURIAN	DEVONIAN	CARBONIFEROU
570 mya	505 mya	438 mya	408 mya	360 mya

CONTENTS

PLIOCENE **5.3 mya**
PLEISTOCENE **1.6 mya**

page 22

page 29

page 34

page 18

The great
extinction that
killed the
dinosaurs

PALEOCENE

EOCENE

OLIGOCENE

MIOCENE

66.4 mya

57.8 mya

36.6 mya

23.7 mya

PERMIAN

TRIASSIC

JURASSIC

CRETACEOUS

86 mya

245 mya

208 mya

144 mya

A fossil trilobite. Trilobites were armored, insect-like animals that swam in the Earth's oceans between the Cambrian and Permian periods. They became extinct about 245 million years ago. This one is from the Burgess Shale, a geological site in British Columbia that was discovered in 1909 by Charles Doolittle Walcott of the Smithsonian Institution.

The past is a puzzle with most of the pieces missing. When we try to reconstruct how creatures lived millions and millions of years ago, we can only make a guess—a guess based on little evidence. The fossil record is scanty. When animals die, soft parts rarely fossilize because they decay quickly or are eaten by scavengers. Usually, the bits of fossilized bone, teeth, scales, and shells that we do find give only hints about the life the animal led. What was the color of a dinosaur's skin or eyes? Did trilobites swarm like insects or lead solitary lives? How smart was a giant ammonite? We don't know and we may never know the answers to such questions.

In the last 500 million years, countless numbers of species have appeared, lived for a time, and then vanished. Some species evolved into new forms, while others died out. But a few managed to survive changes on Earth without changing themselves. Some were tough enough to endure violent shocks to their environment. Others found places to live where little competition or environmental change challenged them. We call these survivors "living fossils." They are windows through which we can see the past.

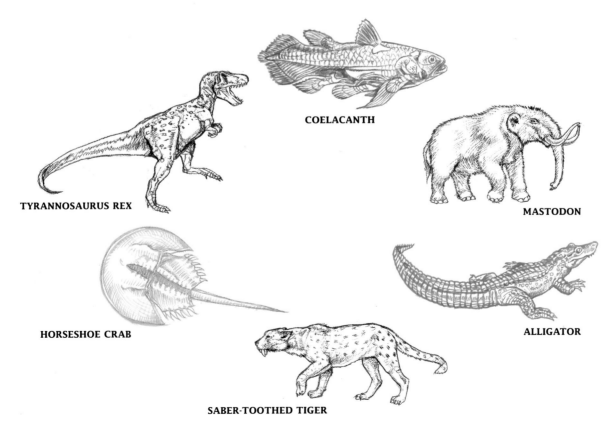

COELACANTH

TYRANNOSAURUS REX

MASTODON

HORSESHOE CRAB

ALLIGATOR

SABER-TOOTHED TIGER

Animals adapt to their environment through natural selection. As the generations pass, their bodies and behavior change slowly. These changes pass to their offspring. Some changes improve the animal's chance of survival; some do not. When animals can't adapt to new conditions, they become extinct.

Changes, called "mutations," occur by accident when genetic molecules become damaged or reproduce incorrectly. For example, sometimes people are born with extra toes. This is a mutation caused by a genetic accident. As far as we know, it doesn't help people in any way. If it did—if, for example, it helped people survive or made us smarter or faster—then those who had it would live longer, and their offspring would have a chance to acquire the trait. And if their offspring did, in fact, acquire the trait, then *their* offspring would have an even better chance of inheriting it, too. It would therefore spread throughout the population after many generations. This is the way new species evolve and earlier designs fade into extinction.

At one time in Europe, the peppered moth lived on lichen-covered trees, where its light coloring provided camouflage. When industrial pollution killed much of the lichen and covered the trees with soot, these light-colored moths became easier for predators, such as birds, to see. Soon peppered moths that were born naturally darker in color began to survive at a more frequent rate, and fewer of the lighter-colored moths lived long enough to reproduce. The darker moths are still found in industrial areas, while the lighter moths are not.

The peppered moth and two darker species of the peppered moth that later evolved.

A painting depicting the impact theory, which suggests that a gigantic asteroid hit the Earth and caused the extinction of the dinosaurs. According to scientists, this asteroid probably hit the Earth in the northwestern Yucatán, in Mexico.

GREAT EXTINCTIONS

Several times in Earth's history, most living things on the planet disappeared. We call these events "great extinctions." One great extinction took place when the dinosaurs (and many other animals and plants) vanished about 65 million years ago. Another occurred just before the dinosaurs first appeared—245 million years ago—when almost 90 percent of the Earth's species died out.

The cause of great extinctions is uncertain. Scientists have suggested volcanic eruptions, drastic climate change, and universal disease as possibilities. According to the most popular theory, called the impact theory, comets or asteroids crashed into the planet, and the impact disrupted the climate enough to kill most life. Craters and other evidence bolster the impact theory.

If a comet hit the Earth, it would trigger earthquakes, volcanic eruptions, tidal waves, and vast fires. Debris and smoke would block the sun for months or even years, and the resulting darkness would kill plants, plankton, and, eventually, the animals that depend on them.

Living fossils avoided change and escaped extinction. They weren't stronger or smarter than other animals; they were simply able to survive. And because of that, they live today, while the dinosaurs do not.

For more than a billion years, jellyfish, worms, and algae dominated the seas. Then, 570 million years ago, the sea suddenly filled with a host of new and strange creatures. Scientists call this the "Cambrian Explosion." The explosion lasted for several million years (which is only a blink in the long history of life on Earth).

Many of the new creatures were protected by armor. The older creatures couldn't attack them or defend themselves. The newcomers flourished.

Opabinia had five eyes and fed with a nozzle. *Hallucigenia* crawled on the sea floor, with long, protective spines guarding its back. *Anomalocaris* was the largest of the new predators. It attacked smaller animals, biting with a circular

mouth that looked like a pineapple slice. And while most animals from this time only grew to be a few inches in length, *Anomalocaris* reached two feet. It was the great white shark of its time.

These creatures lived for a few million years and then disappeared, but one newcomer left a lasting legacy. A *Pikaia* was a simple worm-like creature with a slender spine that wriggled in the mud. It was the first of the chordates, animals with spines, commonly known as vertebrates. Its relatives include fish, dinosaurs, and mammals, including humans.

Because the worm's descendants lived—and *Opabinia* became extinct—today there are many creatures with spines but none with five eyes and a nozzle.

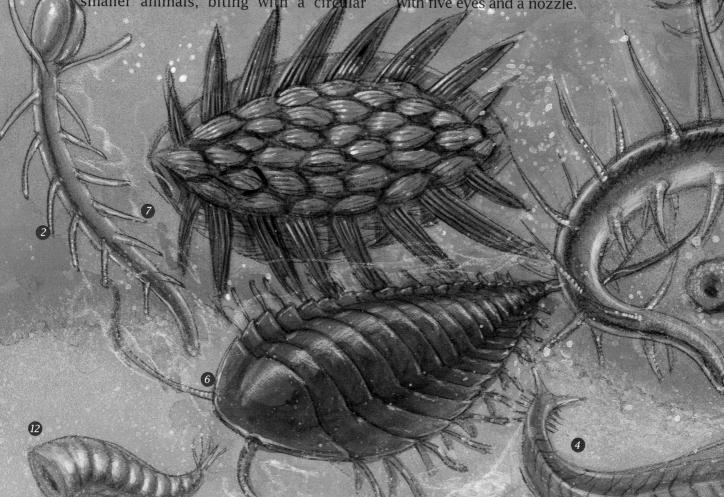

Some of the strange animals of the Cambrian Explosion: *Opabinia regalis (1)*, *Hallucigenia (2)*, *Anomalocaris (3)*, *Pikaia gracilens (4)*, *Ogygopsis (5)*, *Emeraldella (6)*, *Wiwaxia (7)*, *Ottoia prolifica (8)*, an echinoderm *(9)*, *Naraoia compacta (10)*, *Waptia (11)*, an archaeocyathid *(12)*, and *Leanchoilia superiata (13)*.

A fossil sea scorpion, a close relative of the horseshoe crab. Ancient sea scorpions could grow to ten feet in length.

THE HORSESHOE CRAB

At first, the most successful new animals of the Cambrian Explosion were the trilobites—a family of swimming, armored, insect-like animals. They dominated the seas for millions of years. They belong to a group of animals called arthropods, which includes today's scorpions, spiders, and insects. Although trilobites became extinct 245 million years ago, other arthropods thrived. Most animal species alive today are arthropods.

Fossil evidence shows that one early arthropod called the horseshoe crab developed at the same time as the trilobites. About 300 million years ago, in the Carboniferous Period, horseshoe crabs were at their peak. The species of horseshoe crab that lived then differed little from species alive today.

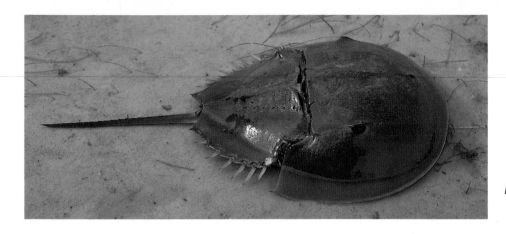

Horseshoe crab.

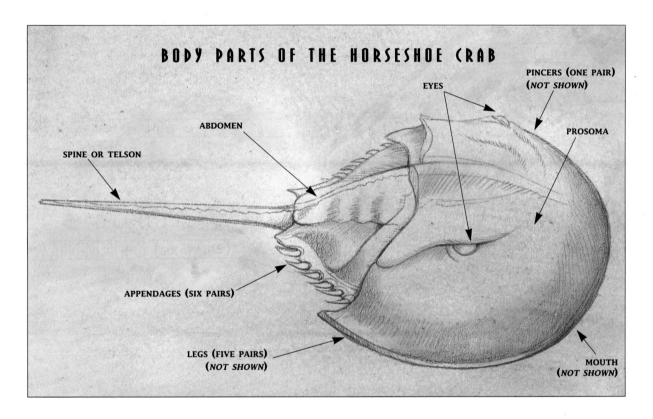

BODY PARTS OF THE HORSESHOE CRAB

PINCERS (ONE PAIR) (*NOT SHOWN*)

EYES

ABDOMEN

PROSOMA

SPINE OR TELSON

APPENDAGES (SIX PAIRS)

LEGS (FIVE PAIRS) (*NOT SHOWN*)

MOUTH (*NOT SHOWN*)

Pill bug.

Horseshoe crabs, in fact, are not crabs at all. True crabs belong to a family called crustaceans, a group of animals that scurry on the sea floor and hide in hollows. Horseshoe crabs more closely resemble pill bugs, a kind of insect. Instead of scuttling across the sea floor, like real crabs, horseshoe crabs swim. Their tiny legs flail at the water from under an armored shell that looks like a submerged tank.

One night each spring, when the sun and moon occupy the same part of the sky, their combined gravity creates an unusually high tide. The female horseshoe crabs allow the tide to carry them high on the beach. The males, all smaller than the females, hitch a ride on their backs. Once on the beach, the females scoop out nests and lay their eggs. The males fertilize them at once. After burying the eggs, the adults hurry after the receding tide. Six weeks later, when the sun and moon produce another high tide, the eggs are immersed in water. The moisture signals the eggs to hatch.

The young horseshoe crabs spend their early years near the beach. Few predators patrol the shallows. At high tide the horseshoe crabs feed on small

Horseshoe crab eggs are small and bead-like.

Horseshoe crab eggs just prior to hatching.

organisms. When the water subsides, they burrow into the sand to await the next high tide and their next feeding. As they grow, they venture into deeper and deeper water. They finally leave the land for good and become fully aquatic. They are ready to mate in five to ten years. Then the moon draws them back to the shore, and the cycle repeats.

Horseshoe crabs are hardy and unfussy. Variations in the saltiness of the water don't disturb them. They eat anything and are the last creatures to suffer from pollution. Although they prefer the water, they can survive for days buried in sand if a high tide strands them.

Despite millions of years of evolutionary adaptations among competing organisms, horseshoe crabs still thrive with their original design. They endured change better than *Anomalocaris, Opabinia, Hallucigenia,* or their cousins the trilobites. Horseshoe crabs outlived them all.

THE NAUTILUS

For 50 million years after the Cambrian Explosion, trilobites feared nothing in the sea. Then, just over 500 million years ago, the first nautilus appeared. With hard shells and sharp beaks, these relatives of octopus and squid found trilobites easy prey.

The earliest nautilus lived in long shells that looked like tall dunce caps. Later species developed spiral shells with striped patterns. The spiral shell protects their soft bodies; only the tentacles, beak, and eyes protrude. At their peak, about 100 million years ago, over 2,500 nautilus species roamed the sea.

As the ages passed, new animal species learned to defeat the nautilus' defenses. The first fish to develop powerful jaws, such as coelacanths and the earliest sharks, crushed their shells. Later, some dinosaurs dove into the sea to feast on the slow-moving animals. Nautilus would never be the top predator of the sea again.

To avoid their pursuers, nautilus dove to the depths of the ocean. They spent their days a thousand feet down, where swimming reptiles couldn't follow and where darkness hid them from hungry fish. Only on dark, moonless nights did they surface in order to feed.

As the nautilus adapted, other creatures did as well, but the adaptations didn't always prove useful. Ammonites were nautilus' relatives. They looked like nautilus, but their internal structure and habits differed significantly. Instead of hiding in the deep, ammonites defended themselves from predators by growing thicker and thicker shells, some covered with spines. Unfortunately, their predators grew larger still.

The event of 65 million years ago that killed the dinosaurs also wiped out the ammonites. Their shells couldn't protect them. If a comet or asteroid did hit the Earth (as many scientists believe), the forests caught fire and the surface of the sea boiled. Then debris and smoke blocked the sun, so the temperature fell.

Why did the nautilus survive while the ammonites disappeared? One theory says that the nautilus were protected because they lived in deep water. Ammonites deposited their eggs in the plankton at the ocean's surface, so that

Ancient nautilus *(1)* and some of the giant predators that lived in the ocean during the Cretaceous Period: the mosasaur *Tylosaurus (2)*, a pliosaur *(3)*, *Archelon*, a ten-foot-long turtle *(4)*, the shark *Scapanorhynchus (5)*, and an ancient herring species, *Portheus (6)*. ➤

Like squid, octopus, and cuttlefish, nautilus are cephalopods. "Cephalopod" means "head-foot." The tentacles, or "feet," come out of the head, waving in front of their primitive eyes. They jet through the oceans by inhaling water and forcing it out of a tube called a siphon. Some cephalopods have a poisonous bite. The blue-ringed octopus can kill a man with a nibble, but the nautilus is harmless. While octopus have suckers, the nautilus depends on a sticky material covering its tentacles to grab and hold food.

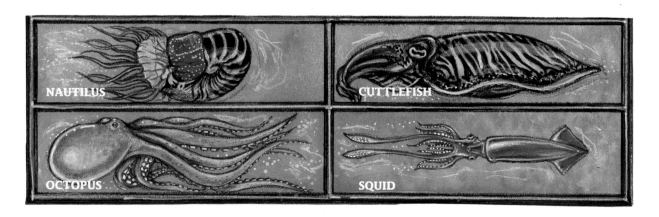

NAUTILUS

CUTTLEFISH

OCTOPUS

SQUID

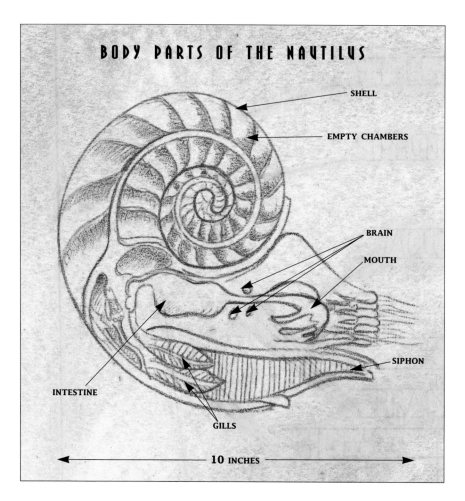

BODY PARTS OF THE NAUTILUS

SHELL

EMPTY CHAMBERS

BRAIN

MOUTH

SIPHON

INTESTINE

GILLS

10 INCHES

Two adult nautilus, photographed in the Pacific Ocean.

the young ammonites could feed when they hatched. Nautilus, on the other hand, left a few sturdy eggs deep in the water. If a large comet hit, high surface temperatures would have killed all the ammonites *and* their eggs, as well as most adult nautilus—but not the nautilus eggs resting safely on the bottom.

Newborn nautilus thus arrived in a depleted world. But many of the nautilus' enemies survived, too. Fish dominated the sea, and predatory mammals such as

dolphins and killer whales adapted to ocean life.

Today, nautilus live in the tropical Pacific Ocean. Only four or five species survive, virtually unchanged from their ancient ancestors. The habits that saved them 65 million years ago keep them alive today. On moonless nights, they come to the surface to feed, eluding fish instead of swimming reptiles, bobbing on the surface like Christmas ornaments.

THE TUATARA

After spending the day at rest, the tuatara pokes its nose out of its burrow as the sun sets. As the temperature dips below 50 degrees Fahrenheit, it begins to hunt. When the temperature drops, most reptiles slow down. Snakes retreat to a snug hole, and even the world's largest lizard, the mighty Komodo dragon, lies low until sunrise. But the tuatara can still move. When chilled, it may breathe only once an hour. Its slow metabolism means it requires little food.

The tuatara looks like a lizard, but it is actually the last survivor of an order of reptiles called Rhynchocephalia, or "beakheads," because their jaw is hooked like a bird's beak. Its earliest predecessor, *Homoeosaurus,* lived in Europe in the Jurassic Period. The first beakheads

A tuatara.

METABOLISM

"Metabolism" refers to the rate at which an organism uses the energy that it gets from food. A small, fast, warm-blooded animal like a hummingbird burns a lot of energy flying and keeping warm. A reptile doesn't burn calories to stay warm. Instead, it basks in the sun or absorbs heat from its environment. It sits around all day and uses little energy except to chase prey. While the hummingbird must eat all day, reptiles eat relatively infrequently. Pound for pound, reptiles need about one-tenth the food of mammals or birds.

COMPARING METABOLISMS	HEARTBEATS	BREATHS
HUMMINGBIRD	500 per minute; over 1,200 per minute when scared	15,000 per hour (at rest); 16,500 per hour (when active)
HUMAN	70–80 per minute	840 per hour
TUATARA	approx. 7 per hour	1 per hour (when cold)

Various metabolic rates are represented by the hummingbird (very fast), the human (average), and the tuatara (very slow). Compare by looking at how often they breathe and how often their hearts beat.

appeared more than 200 million years ago in the Triassic Period.

Tuatara fossils are found on every continent except Antarctica. Modern tuataras live only on a few remote, rocky islands off the coast of New Zealand. New Zealand's Maori natives gave the creature its name, which is pronounced "TOO-UH-TAR-UH" and means "spine-bearer."

Tuataras grow to about two feet in length and weigh about two pounds. Their skulls and skeletons are different from a lizard's. Instead of separate teeth, they have enameled jawbone protruding through their gums. Tuataras have three eyes. The third eye, complete with retina, lens, and nerves to the brain, sits under a transparent scale atop the head. It is not known what purpose this "eye" serves, but it is not used for seeing.

Some tuataras have survived for over 75 years in captivity, and Maori people claim that some live to be 300 years old. Other reptiles with slow habits live a long time, too. For example, Galápagos tortoises live for more than a century.

No one knows why tuataras survived the great extinction that killed off the dinosaurs. Perhaps their sluggishness saved them. With low energy requirements, they would have been able to live in colder climates with reduced oxygen and little food. Perhaps they survived on a few isolated islands because they faced little competition from other animals.

Having survived mass extinctions and 200 million years of evolutionary

A Jurassic landscape, including *Homoeosaurus (1)*, an ancient relative of the tuatara. Also shown are the dinosaurs *Brachiosaurus (2)*, *Camarasaurus (3)*, and *Hylaeosaurus (4)*, the swimming reptile *Plesiosaurus (5)*, and the smallest known dinosaur, *Compsognathus (6)*. In the air are *Archaeopteryx (7)* and *Rhamphorhynchus (8)*.

change, tuataras have been hunted to the verge of their own extinction by rats and other predators introduced to their environment by man. However, the New Zealand government has taken action to save the tuatara. To protect and increase the population, scientists excavate and incubate tuatara eggs in a laboratory. After they hatch, they are released into the wild to survive on their own. The government conducts rat hunts to keep the tuataras safe and forbids people from visiting the islands where they live because their boats may carry rats and other threats.

The tuatara teeters on the edge of extinction, but this energetic rescue program shows promise. Without human help, these will be the final days for beakheads.

THE COELACANTH

As a young girl, Marjorie Courtenay-Latimer played along the seashore on the coast of South Africa, watching the birds and the marine life. As she grew older, she remained fascinated by nature, eventually becoming curator of a natural history museum.

The museum couldn't afford to send her on expeditions, so she made the best of opportunities close to home by asking local fishermen to bring her unusual fish snared in their nets.

In 1938, they brought her an odd-looking 100-pound, five-foot-long blue and silver fish. She had never seen a fish like this one. The local people called it a "great sea lizard" because of its strange fins. It was covered with hard, bony scales, sharp spines, and a slimy oil that oozed from its skin. Although unknown to science, this fish was well known by the local people. They dried and salted it for food and used the scaly skin as sandpaper.

She returned immediately to the museum with her strange find. She sent it to a famous British fish expert. To her astonishment, the expert identified it as a coelacanth (pronounced "SEE-LUH-KANTH")—a fish thought to have been extinct for at least 65 million years! The expert said, "I would hardly have been more surprised if I met a dinosaur on the street!"

Before 1938, the youngest known

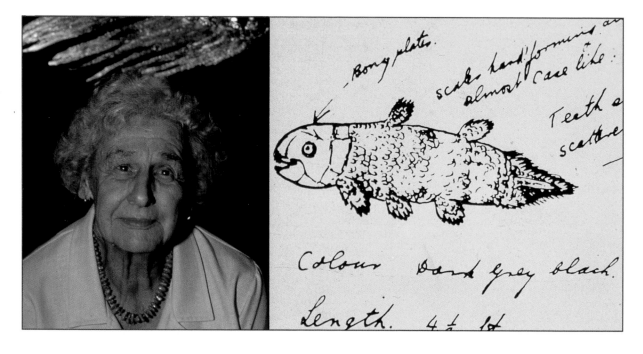

Marjorie Courtenay-Latimer, who rediscovered the coelacanth in 1938, her drawing of the coelacanth, and some of her notes on the discovery.

One of the few live coelacanths ever photographed.

coelacanth fossil was 136 million years old. The professor named the coelacanth *Latimeria chalumnae* after Marjorie Courtenay-Latimer.

The first true coelacanths appeared almost 286 million years ago during the Permian Period, the period preceding the appearance of dinosaurs. However, it was 400 million years ago, in the Devonian Period, when lobe-finned bony fish similar to the coelacanth, along with early sharks and other creatures, put an end to the nautilus' supremacy. Their teeth could crack the nautilus' shell. And they swam fast, so they attacked and escaped quickly, while nautilus could only bob like a cork.

The ocean in the Permian Period, including three coelacanths *(1)*. Also shown are two ancient shark species, *Hybodus (2)* and *Cladoselache (3)*, an ammonite *(4)*, another type of cephalopod called a belemnite *(5)*, and two lungfishes, *Scaumenacia (6)* and *Dipterus (7)*. On the ocean floor is *Diplocaulus (8)*, an ancient amphibian, and several shellfish.

Eventually, coelacanths had to cope with the same problem that forced the nautilus into deep water: larger, more efficient predators filled the seas, such as swimming lizards and dinosaurs, giant sharks, seagoing crocodiles, and new breeds of hunting fish. Like the nautilus, the coelacanths migrated to deeper water.

Today coelacanths live near the Comoro Islands, in the Indian Ocean, hundreds of feet below the surface. Their deep-sea habits explain why scientists didn't notice them for so long—and how they could have survived the impact of a comet or asteroid on the Earth. The earthquakes, tidal waves, fires, and boiling water simply couldn't reach the coelacanths in their cold, dark home. Just as the nautilus may have escaped extinction by placing its eggs in the protective deep, the coelacanths may have survived by living there.

In 1987, when special boats designed for deep diving and observation had become available, scientists observed living coelacanths for the first time. The scientists expected the fish to use their lower fins to crawl across the sea floor. They didn't. Instead, they swam by flailing their fins wildly. The coelacanths also swam backward and belly up. The scientists were surprised to see the fish stand on their heads and remain vertical for minutes at a time. No fossil studies could have revealed these behaviors. It was as though the scientists had been transported back in time and seen *Tyrannosaurus rex* skipping through a field of flowers.

Tests demonstrated that the headstands may help the coelacanths hunt. A special organ in their heads detects the electrical fields that some animals produce. The coelacanths may stand on their heads in order to find prey.

Although we've learned a lot more about living coelacanths in recent years, many mysteries remain. For example, scientists have no idea how long coelacanths live, and their reproductive cycle and mating habits are unknown. Perhaps other relatives of the coelacanth still exist. They may live undiscovered in remote depths far from the Comoro Islands.

Some scientists think mammals evolved from bony fishes like the coelacanth. Lungfish, a modern relative of the coelacanth, uses its fins to crawl on land just as our early ancestor—and the coelacanth's descendant—may have done. When people catch this relic from a lost time in their fishing nets, they come face to face with a distant relative.

Coelacanth found in 1952 by J.L.B. Smith.

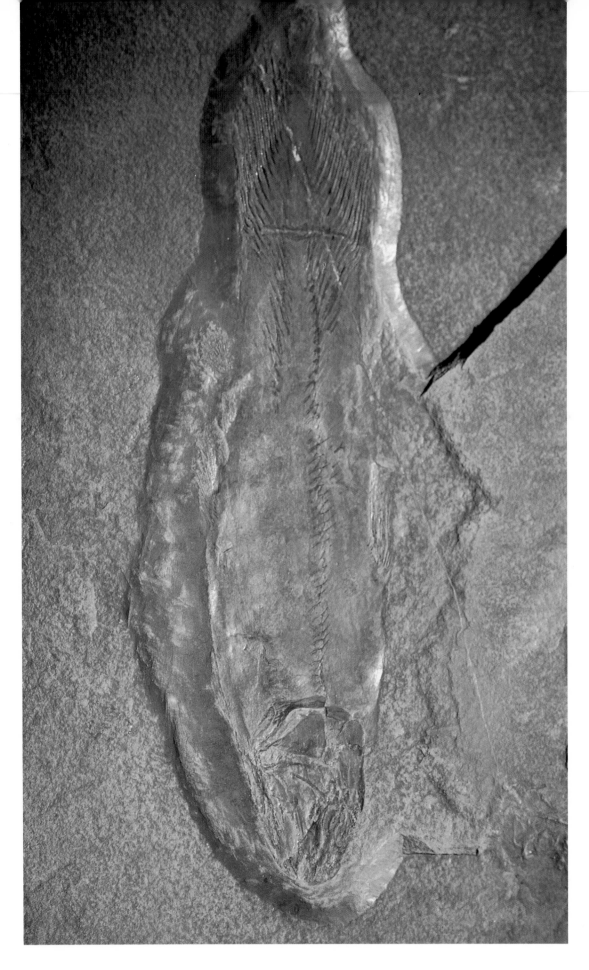

Fossil coelacanth.

Some of the creatures of the Triassic Period, including the giant crocodilians *Deinosuchus* (1), *Desmatosuchus* (2), and *Metriorhynchus* (3). Also shown are *Rutiodon* (4), a member of a crocodilian-like reptile group called phytosaurs; *Nothosaurus* (5); *Plateosaurus* (6); two mammal-like reptiles, *Cynognathus* (7) and *Lystrosaurus* (8); and one of the first mammals, *Megazostrodon* (9). In the water are lungfish (10), ammonites (11), and sea lilies (12).

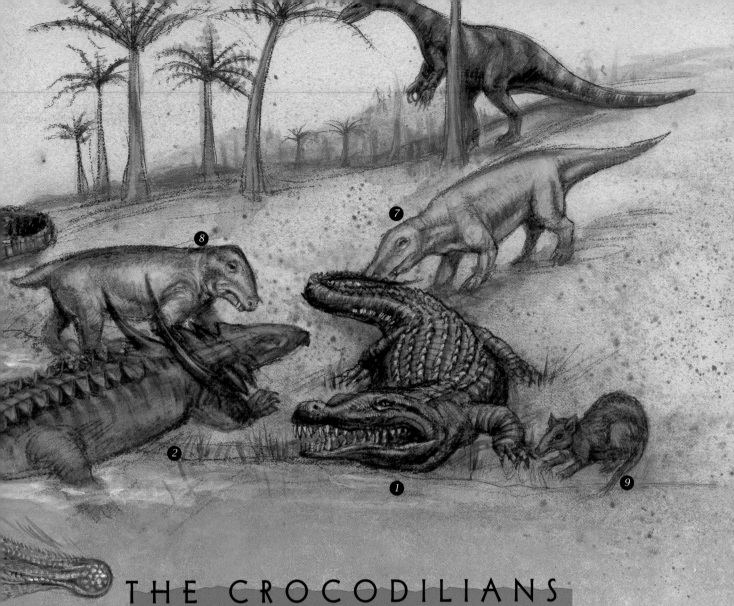

THE CROCODILIANS

Near the end of World War II, Allied forces pinned down a group of Japanese soldiers on Ramree Island, near the Burma coast. The soldiers fled across a tidal swamp at night, trying to escape. More than 1,000 men died. While some drowned or were felled by gunfire, many were killed, and perhaps eaten, by an ancient predator: the saltwater crocodile, among the largest and most dangerous of the crocodilians.

Both crocodiles and dinosaurs first appeared in the Triassic Period, which began about 245 million years ago. An early crocodile relative defended itself with sharp spikes instead of teeth and ate plants, but most species were predators. In the Jurassic Period some crocodilians developed fins and took to the sea, where they preyed on ammonites, nautilus, and other ocean dwellers. By the end of the Cretaceous Period, crocodiles had evolved into many forms. *Deinosuchus,* which means "terror crocodile," grew to 50 feet in length, large enough to make a meal of smaller dinosaurs. Other species measured as little as 16 inches in length. The immense *Stomatosuchus* sucked fish into its gaping duck-billed mouth. Members of the Metriorhynchid family developed fins and a shark-like tail while losing their armor plating.

Twenty-two crocodilian species lurk in the rivers and swamps of the world today. Although none reach 50 feet in length, they are the largest reptiles on Earth. Crocodilians comprise three main groups: crocodiles, alligators and caimans, and gavials. These survivors are almost identical to species that lived 100 million years ago.

Saltwater crocodiles today grow to a maximum of 22 feet, although half that length is more common. The gavial of India (a specialized fish-eating crocodilian) and the Nile crocodile of Africa grow almost as large.

A few crocodiles live in southern Florida and in Venezuela, but alligators,

Crocodiles feeding in Madagascar.

A Nile crocodile from Madagascar.

An American alligator from the southeastern United States.

rather than crocodiles, rule the Americas. Alligators differ from crocodiles in two ways: they tend to have broader snouts, and their teeth are relatively even (the fourth tooth of a crocodile's lower jaw visibly juts above the others). Unlike crocodiles, gators rarely eat people—although pets often disappear in alligator country.

Crocodilians seem smarter than most reptiles. In captivity they recognize their keepers. They show signs of curiosity. Roars, postures, and head movements serve as language. One low-frequency roar causes water drops to dance on their backs from the vibration.

Crocodilians prefer to hunt at night. They surge toward their prey, propelled by a powerful swish of the tail. They drag their victims underwater and spin violently, often tearing the prey apart.

Their night-hunting ability, however, makes them vulnerable to human hunters.

The spectacled caiman of South America, with its glowing eyes.

Their eyes, which are adapted for night vision, reflect light. Hunters find them simply by sweeping a flashlight over the water. The eyes look like two glowing coals.

A closeup of the skin of an American alligator.

Hunters have driven many species of crocodilian to the brink of extinction. Crocodile skin makes excellent leather, and most people are happy to see these dangerous animals removed from their rivers. Conservation efforts have allowed some species, such as the American alligator, to recover, but others may become extinct soon.

Whereas most reptiles lay their eggs and depart for good, crocodilians care for their offspring. After preparing a nest and laying her eggs, a mother crocodilian guards the nest against egg-eating predators. When the eggs hatch, she carries the young to the water in her mouth. They stay near her for a while, sometimes sunning themselves from the safety of her back.

While resting underwater, crocodilian hearts beat only three or four times a minute. The animal can cut the blood supply to its lungs to conserve oxygen. These abilities suggest one reason why crocodilians survived while dinosaurs perished. Crocodilians burn very little energy, so they need little food. A large warm-blooded creature requires ten times as much food as a cold-blooded reptile the same size, because reptiles heat their bodies with sunlight, while mammals create warmth from food. Some scientists believe that certain dinosaurs were warm-blooded. If food became scarce, the more efficient large animals, like cold-blooded crocodilians, could live on low rations while large warm-blooded animals starved.

Crocodile hatchlings in Uganda, in Africa.

THE KOMODO DRAGON

The mother hadrosaur trumpeted in rage. A marauding lizard was eating all her eggs. In swift retribution, the two-ton dinosaur flattened the lizard as it swallowed the last one.

The fossil skeleton of a monitor lizard lying among broken dinosaur eggs was found in Montana recently. But while the hadrosaur vanished 65 million years ago, descendants of the egg thief remain.

The egg thief may have been an ancestor of the Komodo dragon.

Feeding Komodo dragons can quickly strip a carcass to the bone.

The jaw of a Komodo dragon.

The Komodo dragon is the biggest of a group of reptiles called monitor lizards. Adult males can tip the scales at 300 pounds, and they can grow to ten feet in length. Like other monitors, they have extra-long necks, and like snakes, they can unhinge their jaws to eat prey larger than their heads. Curved teeth can rip huge chunks of flesh, and a large, hungry Komodo dragon can eat 100 pounds of meat in a few minutes. Like all monitors, they will eat almost anything they can swallow: cows, pigs, rotting carcasses, smaller dragons, and even people.

Komodo dragons live on four Indonesian islands: Rinca, Flores, Padan, and Komodo, which gives the creature its name. On Komodo, megapode birds make nests out of piles of dirt, and the dragons enjoy digging for the tasty eggs. Their diet makes their breath foul and their bite deadly. Bacteria from the rotten flesh they eat remain in their mouths and infect any animal they bite. So even if an animal escapes a Komodo dragon attack, infection will kill it a few days later if it has been bitten. The Komodo dragon then tracks it down by smell.

Komodo dragons are poor parents. If an adult catches a baby, even its own, it will gulp it down. So after hatching, baby dragons take to the trees. Groups of adult dragons often share a carcass without squabbling, but the young ones shun these meals until they grow large enough to avoid being mistaken for lunch.

A Komodo dragon.

Komodo dragon group, Komodo Island, Indonesia.

The Komodo dragon is the world's largest lizard, but it is not the largest that ever lived. During the Pleistocene Epoch, less than two million years ago, Komodo dragons lived in Australia. They shared their habitat with a large 2,000-pound species of monitor lizard that fed on giant kangaroos and other now-extinct giant marsupials and species such as the pygmy elephant. It probably ate the smaller Komodo dragon as well.

One theory says the Komodo dragon swam away from Australia to escape from the larger, more dangerous reptile and to look for a new home. Some scientists think that when aboriginal people arrived in Australia 40,000 years ago, they may have hunted the giant monitors to extinction, but by then the Komodo dragon had escaped.

As deadly as Komodo dragons can be, they are also fragile. Like the crocodilians, they may have avoided extinction 65 million years ago because of their reptile characteristics—a slow heartbeat and low energy needs. But these same characteristics make it impossible during normal times for dragons to compete with more efficient large mammal predators like tigers or bears. However, on their isolated islands they are the only large predator. Away from the islands, they would be unable to compete for food.

Komodo Island.

THE COCKROACH

Tiny creatures from the distant past have invaded people's homes for ages. They scurry at night on six legs, immune to many poisons and unaffected by high doses of radiation. Their hearing far exceeds a human's. A hard, segmented shell acts as armor. They devour almost anything, sometimes chewing through walls.

They are cockroaches, one of the earliest insects. Insects and other arthropods were among the first animals to live on land. Eons ago, eurypterids, monstrous arthropods resembling giant scorpions, dwelled in the swamps. The biggest ever found, *Pterygotus buffaloensis,* grew to ten feet in length. During the Carboniferous Period, some 300 million years ago, thousands of insects existed, including dragonfly-like creatures that fluttered through the forest on wings two feet across. Only the cockroach survives from that time.

The insect life of the Carboniferous Period included cockroaches *(1)*, giant, scorpion-like eurypterids *(2)*, and dragonfly-like creatures such as *Stenodyctia (3)* and *Meganuera (4)*. Also shown are the amphibians *Pholidogaster (5)*, *Urocordylus (6)*, *Branchiosaurus (7)*, and *Diplovertebron (8)*.

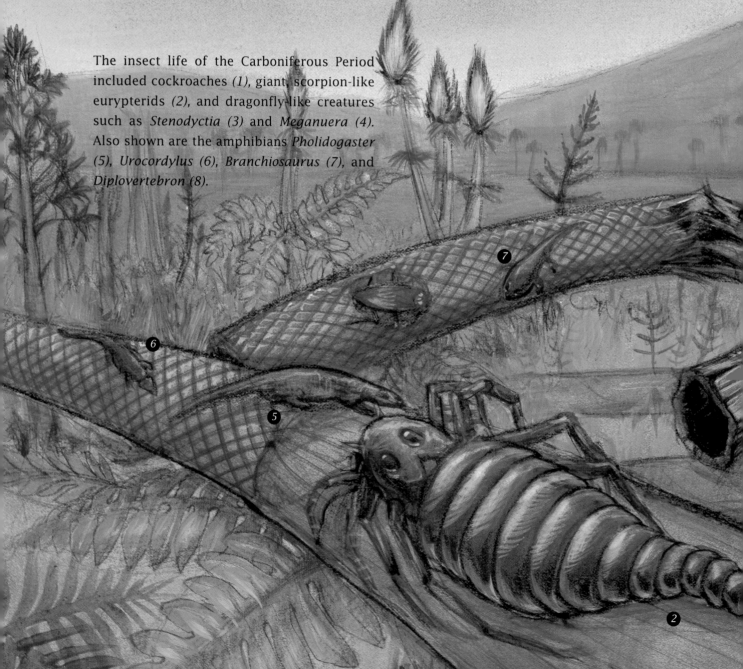

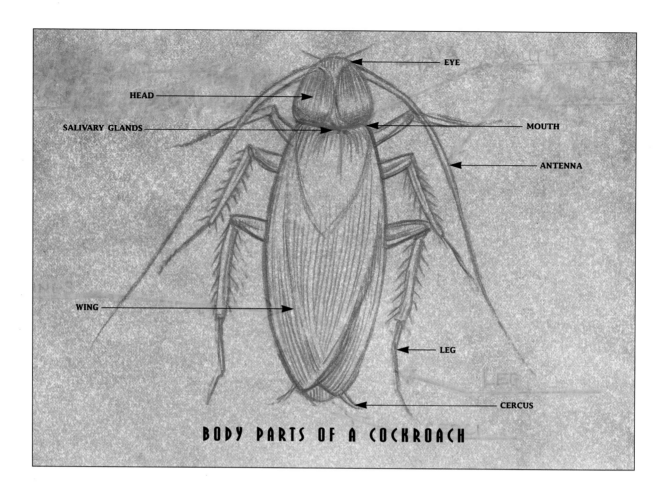

BODY PARTS OF A COCKROACH

Today over 4,000 species of cockroach scuttle about the Earth. Most live in tropical forests. Only a few are household pests.

Cockroaches are complex insects. With training they can learn to solve a maze. They have highly developed senses. They taste their food with chemical-sensitive organs and smell with their antennae. They sport compound eyes like a fly's, with a crystal reflecting layer that allows them to see in dim light. Sensitive hairs around the anus, called "hair sensilla," respond to vibration, including sound. In other words, they hear with their rear ends.

Cockroaches are tough and adaptable,

which is the reason they have survived for so long. A cockroach can live for 30 days without water and three months without food. If you cut off its head, the head can live for half a day by itself.

They will eat almost anything, including the food we like and the packages containing it. They devour camera film and books, petroleum jelly and clothing. Inside their stomachs are teeth for grinding up whatever they consider food. After digestion, they excrete waste through 60 separate tubes. If you unfolded the tubes, they would cover 132,000 square millimeters (204 square inches, or almost 1.5 square feet).

American cockroaches. ➤

The Madagascar hissing cockroach.

The Brazilian cockroach.

Newly hatched cockroaches and their egg case.

◀ *Brazilian cockroaches.*

Many species of cockroach developed unique adaptations. Most insects lay their eggs and abandon them, but cockroaches show motherly care. The mother carries the eggs in a pouch on her rear. One species cares for its young for up to six years. Another produces a sort of milk for its 12 baby roaches to drink. Other species produce many more young. A single German cockroach female can produce 30,000 descendants (including her offspring's young) in just one year.

The hissing cockroach from Madagascar emits its sound by expelling air from its abdomen. (Like all insects, cockroaches breathe through their stomachs.) The hiss is meant to scare the predator, leaving time for the cockroach to escape. This works on birds, but Madagascar is also home to most of the world's chameleons—insect-eating lizards. Unfortunately for the cockroaches, chameleons are deaf, so hissing fails to frighten them.

The hardy cockroach lived through the great extinction that killed the dinosaurs. Instead of being threatened by the works of mankind, they just move in. Tuataras and Komodo dragons also survived some of the same disasters, but only a few of them remain. An epidemic could wipe out the dragons, and an infestation of rats could end the tuatara line. But not the cockroaches. They live almost everywhere, unaffected by change, competition, or disaster. When Mother Nature shuffles the deck again, cockroaches will undoubtedly hold a winning hand and survive to see the new world.

A German cockroach at mealtime.

Dinosaur footprints found in Utah.

The first horseshoe crabs appeared half a *billion* years ago. A creature closely resembling today's Komodo dragon swaggered onto the scene more than 65 million years ago. Human beings, on the other hand, are relative newcomers. Scientists date the earliest recognizable human fossils to only 2 million years ago or thereabouts. But humans have shown amazing adaptability. We live in deserts, jungles, and even in the frozen north.

Despite our success on this planet, we remain fragile. We depend on plant life to create the oxygen we breathe. A large climate change could destroy our crops and herds, which would starve billions. We are as vulnerable to ice ages and comet impacts as the dinosaurs were. Only time will tell if people possess the toughness and adaptability of the living fossils.

INDEX

ammonites, 5, 14, 24, 28, 29
Anomalocaris, 8, 13
Archaeopteryx, 20
Archelon, 14
arthropods, 10

beakheads, 18, 21
belemnites, 24
Brachiosaurus, 20
Branchiosaurus, 40
Burgess Shale, 4

Camarasaurus, 20
Cambrian Explosion, 8, 10, 14
Cambrian Period, 4, 8, 10, 14
Carboniferous Period, 10, 40
cephalopods, 16, 24
chameleons, 45
chordates, 8
Cladoselache, 24
cockroaches, 40–46
   body parts, 42
   breathing, 45
   excretion, 42
   feeding, 42
   intelligence, 42
   Madagascar hissing, 45
   origins, 40, 42
   reproduction, 44
   senses, 42
   toughness, 42, 46
coelacanths, 14, 22–26
   electrical sense, 25
   headstands, 24–25
   origins, 23
   rediscovery, 22–23
   survival, 25
   swimming patterns, 25
Compsognathus, 20
Courtenay-Latimer, Marjorie,
   22, 23
Cretaceous Period, 14, 29
crocodilians, 29–33
   alligators, 30–31, 32
   caimans, 30
   communication, 31
   crocodiles, 30, 31
   Deinosuchus, 28, 29
   Desmatosuchus, 28
   as endangered species, 32
   eyes, 31

crocodilians *(cont.)*
   gavials, 30
   hunting habits, 31
   intelligence, 31
   metabolism, 32–33
   metriorhynchids, 30
   Metriorhynchus, 28
   origins, 29
   reproduction, 32
   Stomatosuchus, 30
crustaceans, 11
Cynognathus, 28

Devonian Period, 23
Diplocaulus, 24
Diplovertebron, 40
Dipterus, 24

eurypterids, 40

Galápagos tortoises, 20
great extinctions, 7, 14

hadrosaurs, 34
Hallucigenia, 8, 13
Homoeosaurus, 18, 20
horseshoe crabs, 10–13, 47
   body parts, 11
   growth, 12–13
   reproduction, 12
   toughness, 13
Hybodus, 24
Hylaeosaurus, 20

impact theory, 7

Jurassic Period, 18, 29

Komodo dragons, 34–39, 47
   feeding, 36, 37
   hunting, 36
   infectious bite, 36
   metabolism, 39
   origins, 38, 39
   young, 37

lungfish, 24, 25, 28
Lystrosaurus, 28

Megamuera, 40
Megazostrodon, 28

metabolism, 19
monitor lizards, 34, 36, 38
   (*see also* Komodo dragons)
mutations, 6

natural selection, 6
nautilus, 14–17, 28
   appearance, 14
   body parts, 16
   defenses, 14
   feeding, 17
   survival, 14, 17
Nothosaurus, 28

Opabinia, 8, 13

peppered moth, 6
Permian Period, 4, 23, 24
Pholidogaster, 40
phytosaurs, 28
Pikaia, 8
Plateosaurus, 28
Pleistocene Epoch, 38
Plesiosaurus, 20
Portheus, 14
Pterygotus buffaloensis, 40

Rhamphorhynchus, 20
Rhynchocephalia, 18
Rutiodon, 28

Scapanorhynchus, 14
Scaumenacia, 24
sea lilies, 28
sea scorpions, 10
Stenodyctia, 40

Triassic Period, 19, 28, 29
trilobites, 4, 10
tuataras, 18–21
   appearance, 19
   as endangered species, 21
   lifespan, 20
   metabolism, 18, 19
   survival, 20–21
   third eye of, 19
Tylosaurus, 14

Urocordylus, 40

vertebrates, 8